College Hill, the president's home—University of Hawaii system

Overleaf: the Manoa campus looking toward Diamond Head, photograph by Gary Hofheimer

The end of the rainbow, Leeward

Previous page: College of Business Administration, Manoa

UNIVERSITY OF HAWAII

A Portrait

University of Hawaii Bookstore

PRINTED IN SINGAPORE

ISBN 0-8248-1460-6

DESIGN, COMPOSITION AND MANUFACTURE OF THIS BOOK
WAS THROUGH THE PRODUCTION SERVICES
PROGRAM OF THE UNIVERSITY OF HAWAII PRESS

PROJECT MANAGER AND EDITOR: WILLIAM HAMILTON

PHOTOGRAPHERS: DAVE AU AND DON SETO
(UNLESS OTHERWISE INDICATED)

DESIGNER: PAULA NEWCOMB

INTRODUCTION

University of Hawaii: A Portrait invites you back to campus—not just to the campus you may have attended but to each of the ten visually and academically distinctive campuses that, taken together, constitute the learning environment of the University of Hawaii. The University of Hawaii is a multi-million dollar "business" employing over 7,000 faculty and staff and educating annually close to 125,000 full-time and part-time students in hundreds of undergraduate, graduate, vocational education, summer school, and community service programs. The next generation of Hawaii's businesspeople, educators, government workers, scientists, technical support people, tradespeople, poets, farmers, and professionals are being educated on campus today.

Founded in 1907 as a land-grant College of Agriculture and Mechanic Arts, the University of Hawaii has evolved into a statewide system composed of a major research university, a four-year campus, an upper division college, and seven community colleges. The ten public institutions are governed by one Board of Regents, whose chief executive officer is the President of the University of Hawaii. Board of Regents members are appointed by the Governor of Hawaii. A brief sketch of each campus follows.

The **University of Hawaii at Manoa,** the founding campus, originally held classes at a temporary downtown Honolulu location (five students made up the first student body) until moving in 1912 to its permanent location. Today the campus is situated on 320 acres in Manoa valley, on the island of Oahu, and serves over 20,000 students. The campus is divided into the central campus (the main instructional site), the makai campus (primarily student dormitories and athletic facilities), and the mauka campus (site of the University of Hawaii Press, the Institute of Astronomy, tropical agriculture sites, and the future site for faculty housing). The University of Hawaii at Manoa shares the responsibilty of undergraduate education with other institutions in the system, but it is the primary site for graduate education, the professional schools, and research.

The **University of Hawaii at Hilo,** founded in 1970, includes a four-year College of Arts and Sciences, a four-year College of Agriculture, and an expanding Center for Continuing Education and Community Service. The campus consists of a 115-acre main campus and the twenty-one acre Manono campus, serving units of the College of Arts and Sciences, the Center for Continuing Education and Community Service, and Hawaii Community College. The school is primarily a residential campus featuring a strong liberal arts focus in all its degree programs. Over 4,500 students attend the University of Hawaii at Hilo.

The **University of Hawaii-West Oahu** is the newest member of the University of Hawaii system. It opened its doors in 1976 as a two-year upper division, liberal arts institution offering junior and senior level courses leading to a baccalaureate degree. Approximately 800 students are enrolled in a wide variety of courses in the humanities, social sciences, and professional studies. The University of Hawaii-West Oahu's administrative and faculty offices are housed in buildings located at Leeward Community College, with whom it shares classrooms. Plans call for a new campus large enough to accommodate a four-year undergraduate program, systemwide research programs and institutional and academic support units.

The seven community colleges offer a rich and varied menu of educational opportunities: basic skills and pre-job or pre-employment preparation; lower division liberal arts courses and specializations in business, food services, health services, public services, and trades and technology. Oahu boasts four of the seven community colleges that serve the diverse needs of island students: Honolulu Community College, Kapiolani Community College, Leeward Community College, and Windward Community College. The remaining three community colleges are located on the islands of Maui, Kauai, and Hawaii. The colleges provide educational services island wide. Maui Community College also provides educational services to Lanai and Molokai.

Honolulu Community College dates back to 1920, when it was established as the Territorial Trade School. It was renamed Honolulu Technical School in 1955, in 1965 it became part of the University of Hawaii, and in 1966 the Board of Regents approved its current name. The college enrolls over 4,500 students and occupies twenty acres on Dillingham Boulevard in the Kalihi-Palama area. In addition to its liberal arts program, it offers the largest number of trade and technical programs in the state.

Kapiolani Community College opened its doors in 1957 as Kapiolani Technical School on a crowded corner lot of the McKinley High School campus. It became a part of the community college system in 1965 and began the move to its present scenic site on fifty-two acres on the slopes of Diamond Head in the mid-1980s. Its extensive set of course offerings, including many vocational programs unavailable elsewhere, makes Kapiolani Community College, with 6,500 students, the community college with the largest enrollment in the state.

Leeward Community College opened in 1968 and immediately attracted vocational students and liberal arts transfer students residing in a previously underserved part of Oahu. The campus, on approximately forty-nine acres, is situated midway between Pearl City and Waipahu and overlooks the middle loch of Pearl Harbor and the Waipio Peninsula. Providing an extensive array of liberal arts programs, vocational education, and community service programs, the campus is heavily utilized day and night by students and the central Oahu community. Leeward Community College serves over 6,000 students in its regular credit program.

Windward Community College, nestled at the foot of the Koolau Mountains on sixty-four verdant acres in Kaneohe, opened its doors in 1972. In addition to the variety of liberal arts and vocational education courses that enroll over 1,700 students, the college prides itself on the vast array of public affairs forums and cultural presentations offered each year. Windward Community College is seen as a major educational asset to the Windward Oahu community.

Maui Community College was founded in 1931 as Maui Vocational School. In 1958 it changed its name to Maui Technical School and in 1966 it was renamed Maui Community College. The college is the only public institution serving the postsecondary needs of students on Maui, Lanai, and Molokai. Occupying seventy-one acres in Kahului, the school offers a unique blend of liberal arts courses; vocational education programs; and, through its two-way audio–video teleconferencing network, courses that reach students at remote sites on Maui and Molokai. Over 2,500 students are enrolled in the regular credit program.

Kauai Community College, on 159 wide-open acres, is one of the system's largest campuses. Founded in 1928 as Kalaheo Vocational School the school is the sole provider of post-secondary education on the island. Name changes took place in 1943 (Kauai Vocational School), 1952 (Kauai Technical School), and 1965 (Kauai Community College). The school serves as the education and cultural center on Kauai, enrolling close to 1,500 students.

Hawaii Community College has an interesting history. The forerunner of the college was the Hawaii Vocational School, established in 1941. It was renamed Hawaii Technical School in 1956 as it expanded its technical training programs. It became Hawaii Community College in 1970 when it merged with the University of Hawaii at Hilo. From 1970 to 1990 the college was part of the University of Hawaii at Hilo. Then in 1990 the college was separated administratively; it now operates as an independent system college. The newly independent school, with an enrollment of approximately 1,900, continues to share facilities with the University of Hawaii at Hilo.

University of Hawaii: A Portrait celebrates through photographic images the natural beauty and the physical beauty that are an integral part of the personality and character of each campus. The natural beauty is experienced through the extensively landscaped campuses, which are an amalgam of native and introduced tropical plants, flowers, and trees. Hawaii's climate keeps the campuses a veritable rainbow of colors year round.

The physical beauty is seen in the diverse architecture and the impressive and expressive artwork found throughout the campuses. Over the years prominent local and internationally recognized architects have been commissioned to design buildings that complement the surrounding environment. Well-known architects such as Charles W. Dickey, I. M. Pei, Clinton Ripley, Arthur Reynolds, and Vladimir Ossipoff have designed many of the distinctive campus buildings. Artists such as John Charlot, Alexander Liberman, and Tony Smith have brought their artistic genius to life in the murals and sculptures found throughout the campuses. Thanks to the foresight of the Hawaii state legislature, Hawaii became the first state in the nation to adopt an Art in State Buildings Law. Passed in 1967, the law requires that one percent of new state building construction funds be set aside for permanent or relocatable artworks. The intent of the law is to enhance the aesthetic quality of public buildings and their spaces, to develop Hawaii's artists, and to expose residents to nationally and internationally known artists. One has only to walk through any of the campuses to appreciate the direct result of the law.

The book captures photographically the diversity and uniqueness of the university campuses as they stand today. In addition, it also records on film several internationally recognized research programs located at sites throughout the state. From the peaks of Mauna Kea and Haleakala to the depths of the surrounding ocean floor, and on the land masses in between, University of Hawaii professors and researchers are uncovering new information to bring into the classroom—information that will be disseminated globally as the university continues its mission to increase knowledge through education.

The theme of the book is campus life. Each image triggers memories of the "good old" college days—days that, for graduates now in the workforce, are fondly remembered and went by all too quickly.

Fortunately, college days never have to end. The University of Hawaii serves the educational needs of those wishing to continue (or start) their college education. Its student body, composed of all age groups, take courses on every topic imaginable. For those unable to attend regular daytime programs, the flexibility of higher education allows a full-time working person to enroll in degree-granting programs offered in the evening or on weekends, to take noncredit courses through Continuing Education or Summer School, or to attend public lectures in the evening. Courses are offered from early morning to late at night. Our thirst for knowledge is timeless. And the University of Hawaii makes knowledge timely.

You are invited to embark on this visual journey through the University of Hawaii campuses. Each image and each page is intended to provide warm memories and instill the desire to view the University of Hawaii as a place you want to return to or become acquainted with for the first time. View with pride the University of Hawaii, which enables students to earn a wide array of degrees—from certificates and associate degrees in more than fifty occupational areas, to associate degrees in liberal arts, to bachelor's degrees in eighty-eight programs, to master's degrees in eighty-five fields, to doctoral degrees in forty-nine specializations, among them the M.D. and J.D. degrees. Enjoy.

Acknowledgments

Many people were involved in the creation of this book. Wayne Fujishige, director of the University of Hawaii Bookstore, conceived of the idea for this book. Ralph Horii, University of Hawaii Vice-President for Finance and Operations, provided administrative support and guidance for the book from the outset. Don Seto and Dave Au turned Wayne's idea into a photographic reality. As often happens in projects of this sort some unexpected visual gaps existed as the book neared completion. Bruce Carlson, director of the Waikiki Aquarium, and Richard Wainscoat, researcher at the Institute of Astronomy, graciously provided photographs of their facilities. Victor Kobayashi, dean of the University of Hawaii at Manoa Summer Session, kindly allowed me to liberally select and use material from his interesting and highly readable book, *Building a Rainbow: A History of the Buildings and Grounds of the University of Hawaii's Manoa Campus*. Janet Heavenridge and Paula Newcomb of the University of Hawaii Press displayed once again their consummate production and design skills. They were able to take the book from very rough form, put all the pieces together, and present the university community with a cohesive, beautifully designed book that is a pleasure to read and view. My heartfelt thanks to all.

WILLIAM HAMILTON

The "Quad," Manoa

Modes of transportation

Hurry up and wait

Books and supplies—a necessary expense

Coconut Island in Kaneohe Bay conducts research in marine biology and related topics

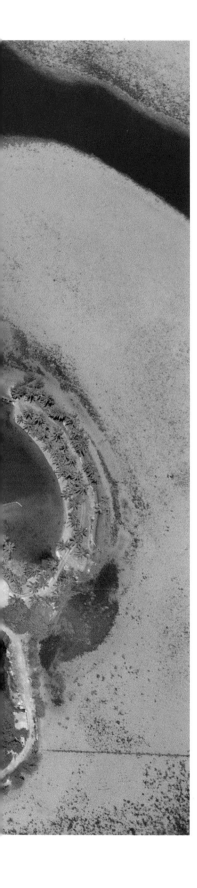

George Hall, Manoa

A botanical delight

Kennedy Theatre, Manoa

"The play's the thing," photographs by James R. Brandon

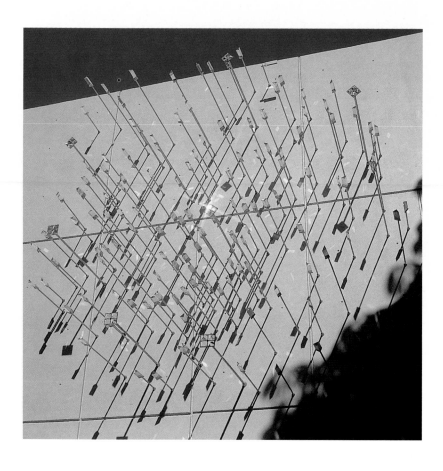

A daytime light show—Otto Piene's *Pleiades* at the Institute of Astronomy is made up of over 150 prisms mounted on stainless steel rods

Observing the universe, the Mauna Kea observatories

On top of the world

International cooperation: the Canada–France–Hawaii telescope, photographs by Richard Wainscoat

A rainy day, Hilo

Playing fetch and catch under the Tony Smith sculpture,
The Fourth Sign, Manoa

Diamond Head as seen from Holmes Hall, Manoa

Bamboo garden in Sakamaki Hall, Manoa

Combining architecture and aesthetics, Kauai

Culture and art, Leeward

A slightly weathered Founders' Gate lines the two sides of
University Avenue at Dole Street, Manoa

Words of scientific wisdom, Bilger Hall, Manoa

Overleaf: A place to study and appreciate art, Hamilton Library, Manoa

Center for Korean Studies, Manoa

Ho'olana, the work of noted Honolulu-based artist, Bumpei Akaji,
stands at the entryway to the library, Hilo

Lunchtime's most popular campus spot, Windward

Dusk at Kapiolani Community College

Campus Center mural, Manoa

In the shadow of the Koʻolau Range, Windward

A pastoral setting, Windward

On the go

Rest and relaxation

Outside looking in . . .

. . . and inside looking up, Biomedical Science Building, Manoa

The audience . . .

. . . the play, Leeward

A relaxed way to study

Checking class notes

Overleaf: Solar, lunar, and satellite research is conducted in Science City atop Haleakala, Maui—the site of several independent research facilities operated by NASA, the FAA, the Air Force, University of Hawaii, and in a collaborative observatory operated by astronomers from University of Hawaii, Purdue University, and University of Wisconsin

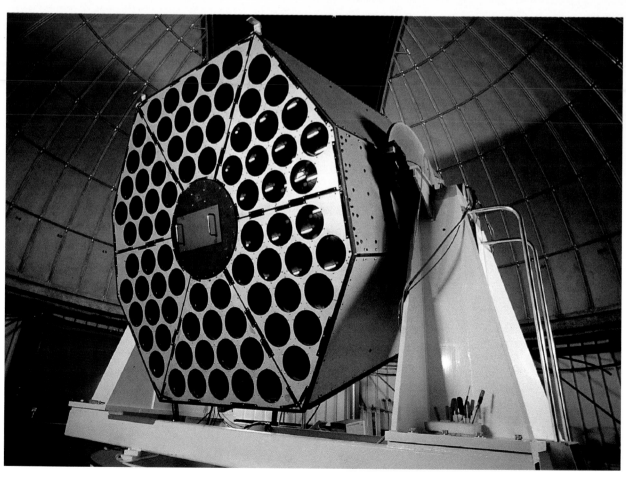

Food and art at Kapiolani

Porteus Hall, Manoa

Night . . .

. . . and day, McCarthy Mall, Manoa

Checking the "score" outside the Music Building, Manoa

Contemplation, the Art Gallery, Manoa

A solar diamond ring, photographs by Richard Wainscoat,
Institute of Astronomy

Mauna Kea is eclipsed

The taro patch, Manoa

Towers of learning, Honolulu

Portal of light, Leeward

Liquid sustenance

St. John Plant Science Laboratory, Manoa

Lighting up the night, Kapiolani

The West Maui mountains appear to be on the campus doorstep

The brain trust, Bachman Hall, Manoa

A gathering of students

Hina-O Na Lani guards the north entryway, Manoa

Hawaii Hall, the University's first permanent building, Manoa

Varney Circle fountain, Manoa

Lyon Arboretum, deep in the Manoa Valley

Cruising through campus

The three-story-high stained-glass entrance to Keller Hall, Manoa

The *Hawaii Peace Memorial* is dedicated to the first Japanese laborers in Hawaii, Manoa

Surf's up near the Pacific Biomedical Research Center at Kewalo Basin, photograph by Tsuyoshi Nakajima

The Aquarium's living reef exhibit, photograph by Thomas Kelly

Tunnel vision

Alexander Liberman's sculpture, *Gate of Hope*, Holmes Hall, Manoa

Out of the classroom for the fieldwork

Finding their way, Kauai

Overleaf: The greenhouse in full bloom, Maui

Geometric patterns, Hilo

The Edwin Mookini Library and Media Center houses over 160,000 bound volumes, Hilo

Can't see the buildings for the trees, Kauai

Spirit Way was created in 1987 by artist Sean K. L. Browne for
Kapiolani Community College

Dolphin was a class project of teacher, John Ringer, and
student welders/artists, Linlee Boulet, Eric T. Sato, and Gwen Brush, Maui

A pleasant place to rest, study, or visit, Maui

Tennis, anyone?, Manoa

Making the turn, Duke Kahanamoku Pool, Manoa

Solitude

Kauai's "gift-wrapped" building

The lush vegetation outside Krauss Hall, Manoa

Gilmore Hall, Manoa, houses—what else—entomology

The Theatre Building is rock solid, Hilo

A creative endeavor

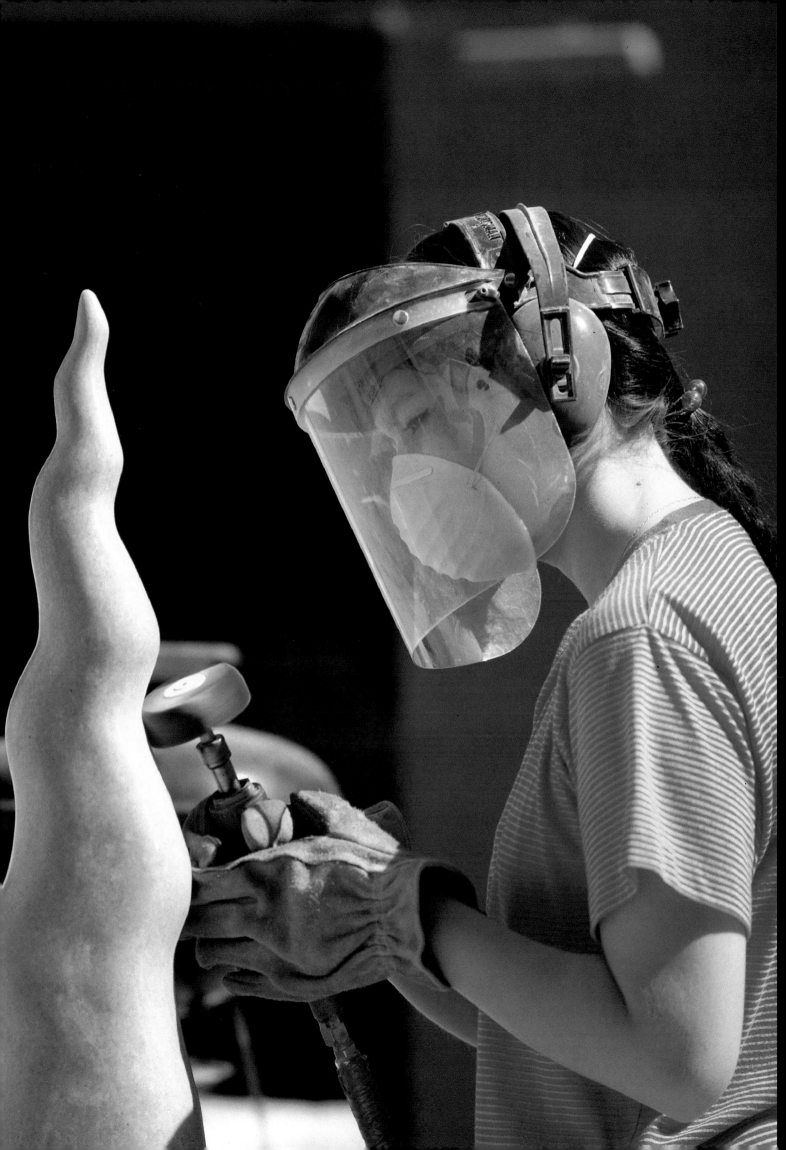

Gone to pot

The Art Building's artistic walkway, Manoa

Clean lines, Honolulu

Student habitat, Manoa

Overleaf: The Aquarium, on the shores of Waikiki (inset photo by Thomas Kelly)

Hitting the books

The interior lighting provides a silhouette effect

The John Charlot frescoes greet visitors to Bachman Hall, Manoa

The pond fronting Krauss Hall, Manoa

An offer too good to pass up

Sakamaki Hall, Manoa

Artistic expression

Study break

Fore! On the "Quad," Manoa

The Makai Campus, Manoa

Runners in scoring position

"I object to this picture, your Honor!"
Richardson Law School, Manoa

Living in the round

Overleaf: Pomp and circumstance

Graduation day

Happiness is a college diploma

"Mom, Dad—I made it!"

The graduate and her proud family

Aloha